The Art of Sugarcraft

ROYAL ICING

The Art of Sugarcraft

ROYAL ICING

BRENDA PURTON

Foreword Desmond Barton
Series Editor Joyce Becker
Photography Graham Tann

MEREHURST PRESS
LONDON

Published 1987 by Merehurst Press
5 Great James Street
London WC1N 3DA

ISBN 0 948075 53 8

Designed by Carole Perks
Editorial Assistant Suzanne Ellis
Typeset by Filmset
Colour separation by Fotographics Ltd, London-Hong Kong
Printed by New Interlitho S.p.A., Milan

ACKNOWLEDGEMENTS

I would like to dedicate this book to my past, present and future students for all the wonderful friendship and support given to me over the years. My great thanks go to Terry, Teresa and Michael, my mother and family, Desmond Barton, Jenny, Doug and all at Mathews, Nicholas Lodge and Bobbie Lane for all their encouragement at all times and to all who have made this book possible for me at Merehurst. Also I wish to thank Tate & Lyle.

The Publishers would like to thank the following for their help and advice:
Lucy Baker
Cuisena Cookware Limited
Kim Golding
Guy Paul and Company Limited, Unit B4, A1 Industrial Park, Little End Road, Eton Scoton, Cambridgeshire, PE19 3JH
B.R. Mathews, 12 Gipsy Hill, Upper Norwood, London SE19 1NN

Companion volumes:

The Art of Sugarcraft — **CHOCOLATE**
The Art of Sugarcraft — **MARZIPAN**
The Art of Sugarcraft — **PIPING**
The Art of Sugarcraft — **SUGAR FLOWERS**
The Art of Sugarcraft — **SUGARPASTE**
The Art of Sugarcraft — **PASTILLAGE AND SUGAR MOULDING**
The Art of Sugarcraft — **LACE AND FILIGREE**

CONTENTS

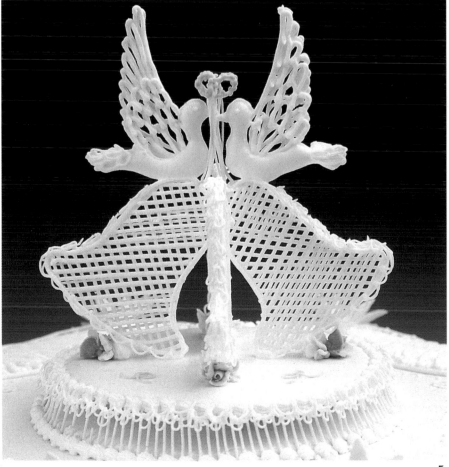

EQUIPMENT

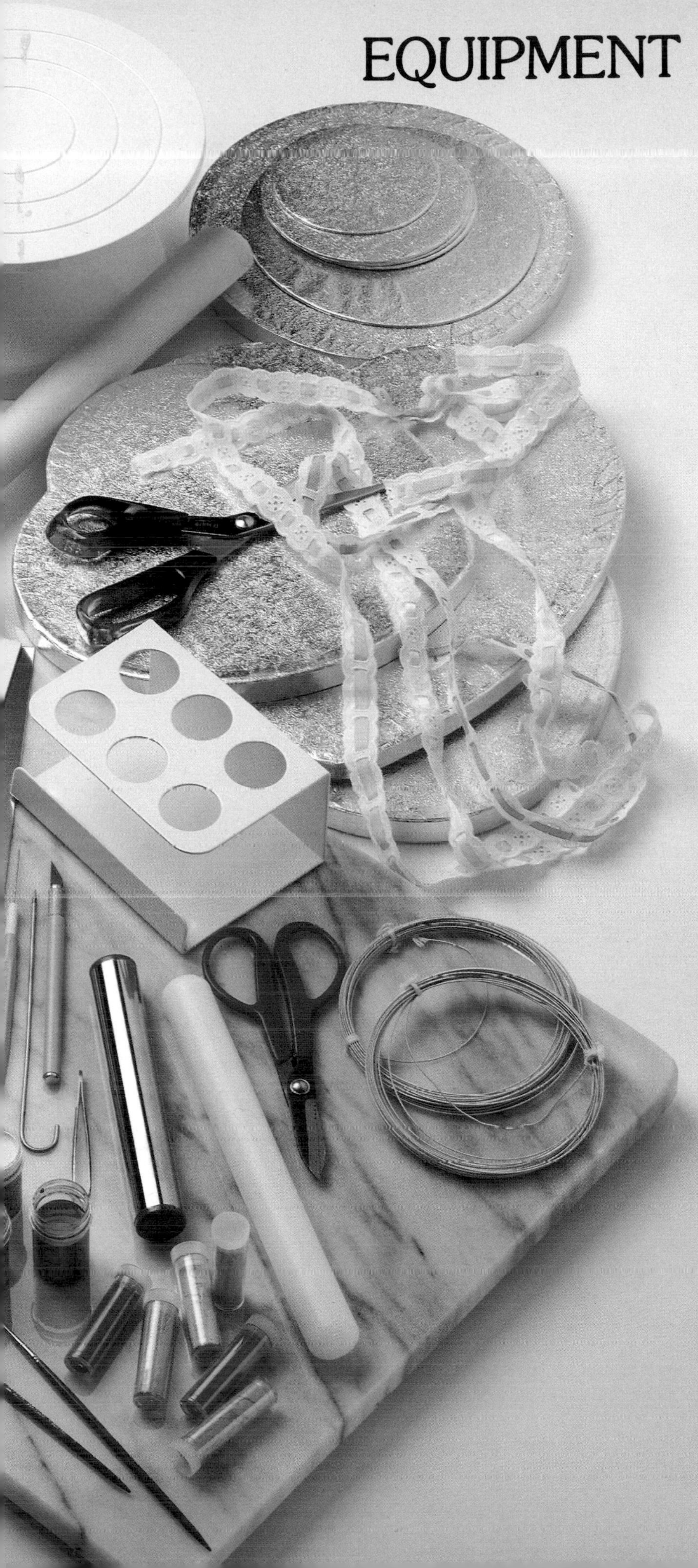

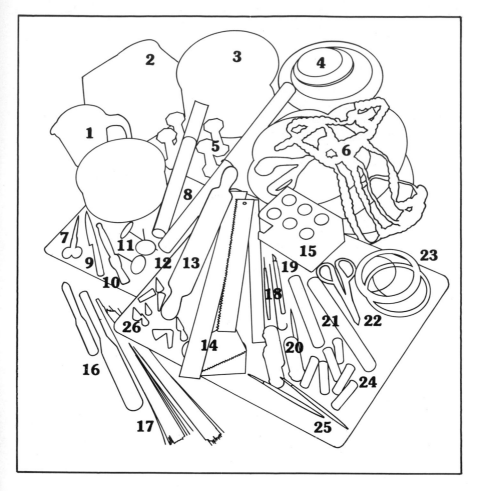

This is a selection of tools and equipment used for royal icing work. Most are ordinary kitchen or household items, while the more unusual tools are available from cake decorating shops and specialist suppliers.

1 Measuring jug
2 Cake tins and pans
3 Turntable
4 Cakeboards and cards
5 Pillars for tiered cakes
6 Ribbons
7 Small and large scissors
8 Greaseproof and wax paper
9 Sharp kitchen knife
10 Pastry brush
11 Flower nails
12 Small and large workboards
13 Large rolling pin
14 Icing ruler, scraper and combs
15 Icing bag stand
16 Palette knives
17 Covered floristry wire
18 Scribers
19 Modelling knife
20 Tweezers
21 Nonstick rolling pins
22 Wire cutters
23 Milliner's wire
24 Paste colours and petal dust
25 Paintbrushes
26 Piping tubes

EQUIPMENT

Most tools used for royal icing are ordinary kitchen equipment. The more specialist tools can be found in a good cake decorating shop.

Mark all tools if you attend classes as most students have the same equipment.

Have a bowl and spatula especially for icing as these must be totally free of any fat.

The turntable should be heavy and strong as it makes coating and piping much easier.

☐ Plain and serrated plastic side scrapers for putting royal icing onto the sides of cakes.

☐ Straight edge for measuring and for evening out royal icing on the top of the cake.

☐ Icing bag stand — this keeps the worktop clean.

☐ Small stainless steel palette knife — this is used constantly in cake decorating for smoothing, trimming, easing runouts off cellophane etc.

☐ Measuring jug.

☐ Glass or earthenware bowl for mixing icing.

☐ Electric mixer for making icing.

☐ Wooden spatula for mixing icing.

☐ Icing tubes — have a good selection and keep them clean with a soft brush.

☐ Sable paintbrushes

☐ Paste colours and petal dust for colouring icing and dusting flowers and runouts.

☐ Silver snowflake dust for giving cakes a sheen.

☐ Milliner's and florist's wire for basket handles and wired flowers.

☐ Thin ribbons for broderie anglaise, baskets etc.

☐ Artist's palette for drying or mixing colours. A worktop could also be used.

☐ Rolling pin, preferably nonstick, for rolling out marzipan and sugarpaste.

☐ Rose nail — flowers are piped onto these.

☐ Basket nail for making baskets. Any small round object could be used.

☐ Cake boards and cards. 10cm (4in) and 12.5cm (5in) round cards.

☐ Drawing pins for pinning patterns to runout boards, templates to cakes etc.

☐ Cellophane or roasting wrap.

☐ Waxed and greaseproof paper — these are used for making templates, patterns etc.

☐ Wire cutter.

☐ Marble slab or other work surface — a cool nonstick surface for rolling out.

MAKING ROYAL ICING

2 large or 3 medium egg whites
approximately 450g (1lb/4 cups)
icing (confectioner's) sugar

Use eggs at room temperature.
Break the white carefully into a
clean bowl and leave to liquify.
Make sure no yolk gets into the
egg white as this will make the
icing heavy and yellow.

The icing sugar should be
fresh, dry and free of lumps. If
there are lumps, put it through a
spotlessly clean sieve.

Add 5ml (1tsp) glycerine at
room temperature when icing has
reached full peak to prevent it
from setting too hard. Add it just
before use. For softer icing use
more glycerine. However
glycerine must not be used when
making piped flowers, runouts or
lace as they will not set hard
enough.

Mixing by hand
All utensils for making royal icing
must be spotlessly clean.
Place egg whites in a clean bowl.
Beat half of the icing sugar in well,
then add the rest a little at a time,
until full peak is reached. Scrape
the sides of the bowl down well
with a plastic scraper.
Beat by hand for about ten
minutes. By this time the icing
should be light and fluffy and able
to hold its shape.
Store at room temperature in an
air-tight plastic container.

Electric mixer method
If making royal icing with an
electric mixer, set at the slowest
speed and use a beater. Work as
for hand mixing, beating for a few
seconds each time a little sugar is
added. It should take about four
minutes all together. Scrape the
sides of the bowl frequently with
the plastic scraper.

Using powdered egg white
Royal icing made from powdered
egg white is whiter and easier to
work with as it sets quickly and
hard. Use 15ml (3tsp) powdered
egg white and 37.5ml (2½fl oz/
⅓ cup) cold water to 450g
(1lb/4 cups) icing sugar. Stir the
powder into the water, then make
the icing by either of the methods
described. Add a little extra sugar
or egg white if necessary to
achieve the right consistency.

COLOURING ICING

The overall appearance of a cake is greatly enhanced by the correct use of colour. Therefore a basic knowledge of the colour spectrum and the way in which colours complement each other is useful.

The spectrum is the range of colours as seen in a rainbow; by mixing these basic colours an infinite range of shades is obtained. When selecting colour for royal icing, take care to choose colours which look edible.

Start by adding a touch of colour to the royal icing; you can build the colour up gradually. Confectioner's colour is usually concentrated colour in liquid, dust or paste form.

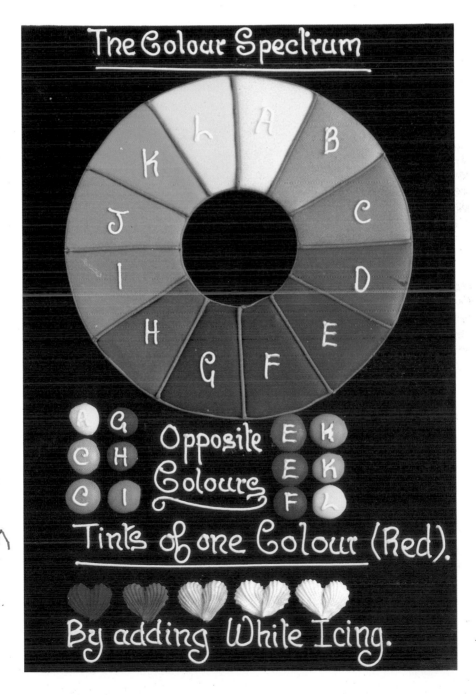

The Colour Spectrum

Opposite Colours

Tints of one Colour (Red).

By adding White Icing.

The easiest colour scheme to use is monochrome, where only one colour is employed, preferably from the warmer side of the spectrum (yellow — orange — red). Use a very light shade for the base coat, a slightly stronger shade for piping shells, scrolls, etc and then a stronger tint still for fine piping, flowers, etc.

The second method is to use contrasting or complementary colours. Here colours opposite each other on the spectrum are used, for example yellow and violet. Again, the colour should be built up from light tints, say pale yellow, for the base with a small quantity of violet added. Do not use equal amounts of the two colours or the cake will look hectic.

The most complicated colour scheme is harmony, which is achieved when three to six colours next to each other on the spectrum are used. Most of the colour should be pastel, with a few darker tints.

Neutral colours such as cream, biscuit, coffee, or chocolate can also be used to great effect. A small amount of neutral colour in any of these methods will enhance the overall appearance. White is a most effective colour to use on cakes.

When adding foliage to piped flowers, the most realistic green is obtained by adding true green to the coloured icing used for the flowers. If the flower colour is very deep, first make it lighter by adding white royal icing, then add the green.

Cameo colours are made by adding a touch of black to pink, green or blue.

The flowers on these practice boards illustrate monochrome, complementary and harmony colour schemes. The numbers refer to the tubes used to pipe the flowers.

LITTLE GIRL CAKE

The little girl runout plaque on this
eighteenth-birthday cake could be
removed and kept as a souvenir of the
occasion.

COATING THE CAKE

It is essential to get a smooth flat iced surface, so be sure the marzipan has been properly applied.

Prepare the royal icing. Colour may be added just before icing. Put the paste in gradually using a cocktail stick or similar to obtain the desired shade. Keep the icing in the bowl covered with a damp cloth at all times to prevent crusting.

Place the cake on a turntable. Using a palette knife put icing on the top. With the knife, spread the icing over the cake, working with a paddle movement to eliminate bubbles. At the same time slowly rotate the turntable with the other hand. When the

icing is evenly spread take the cake off the turntable and place on a worktop.

Place a metal straight edge at the edge of the cake away from you and at an angle of about 45° to the surface. Draw it across the cake in one continuous movement. Move the straight edge backwards and forwards across

the cake until the top is flat.

Remove any icing from the side of the cake and leave the cake to dry in a warm place.

When the top is dry, ice the sides. Put the cake on the turntable. Spread the icing around the sides working from bottom to top with a paddling motion. Slowly rotate the turntable at the same time. Hold the scraper towards you at an angle of about 15° against the side of the cake. With the other hand, slowly rotate the turntable in one continuous movement all the way round then pull the scraper off towards yourself.

A takeoff mark will be left which can be scraped down with a knife when dry.

Give the cake two to four coats of icing, drying and smoothing completely between each. Remove any loose icing before adding another coat. Coat the cake board each time.

A softer royal icing can be used for the final coat if wished. Leave the cake to dry thoroughly before decorating.

If a scroll or shell border is to be used, the top and sides may be iced at the same time. For runout borders or small shells a sharp edge is needed so do the sides at least eight hours after the top.

Place the corner on the point of
the right angle, making a cone.

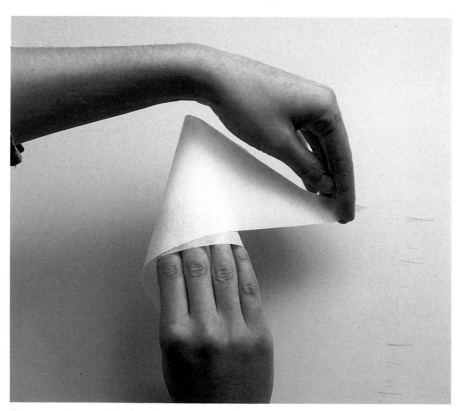

Put your fingers in the cone to
hold it and bring the other corner
over it.

Wrap the corner around the cone
twice so that the points meet.

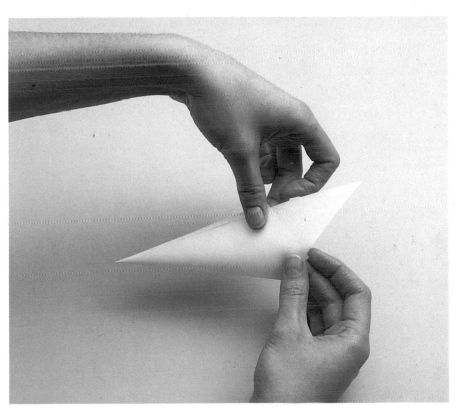

Slide the three points together to
tighten the bag.

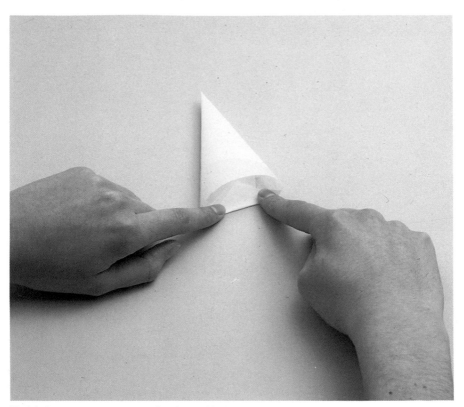

Fold the top point into the bag. If piping without a tube, fill the bag now.

If using a piping tube, cut off the tip of the bag with scissors and insert the tube.

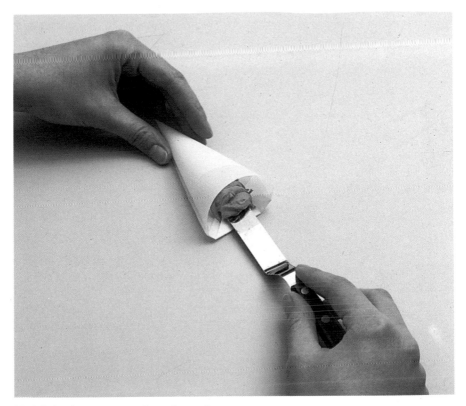

Hold the bag in your hand or place on the table and hold the point. Scoop up some icing with a palette knife and place in the bag.

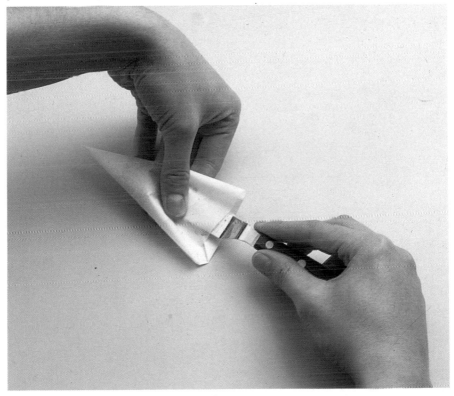

Hold the top of the bag down and gently pull out the palette knife.

Fold the points of the bag towards the centre.

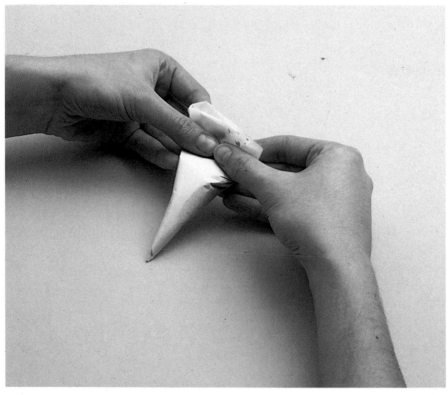

Fasten by folding the top of the bag over twice.

LINES

To give strength to icing used for these techniques add 15ml (3tsp) of powdered egg white to 50ml (2fl oz/¼ cup) water and 450g (1lb/4 cups) icing. Beginners should start with linework to get the feel of the icing and bag and to train their hand in getting the correct pressure. Press, stop pressing, pull down. This will become a natural action. Lines may be overpiped and built up for more elaborate effects.

Fine and bold straight lines can be piped with any writing tube. Place the tube on the cake or practice board, press slowly and evenly and hold in position about 2.5cm (1in) above line required. Let the icing drop into place for about three-quarters of the line. Stop pressing before the end of the line, as enough icing will be left in the action to ease the line onto the cake. Touch down gently taking the tube off. You will have a clean line without a large blob at the end.

THREE-TIER WEDDING CAKE

A classic pink and white round three-tier wedding cake with an exquisite freestanding top ornament.

PRACTICE SHEETS

Use icing at full peak with air bubbles paddled out. Sit comfortably holding the icing bag easily in your hand. Relax your hand and arm. Start by piping straight lines following the practice board on page 33. The lighter lines are piped with a No1 tube, the darker lines with a No0. Hold tube in an upright position; press, stop pressing, pull down. This sequence is used for most piping actions.

1. Scroll piped with No 46, over-piped with white in No1 and graduated dot piped in mauve with No0.

2. Plain scroll and dot.

3. Two scrolls piped facing.

4. Facing scrolls plus overpiping and trellis made with No0 tube.

5. Scroll plus overpiping with No59. To pipe the frill at the base, pleat as you pipe with the thick side of the tube touching the cake, fine side outwards.

6. Extending star piped with No 46. Press, stop pressing, pull out. Pipe star with No43 tube under large ones. Overpipe first with white done with No1, then mauve with No0. Pipe loop from small star, then loop from every other large star.

7. Extending star piped with No46 with star piped with No43 at base. The loop is piped with a No0 tube.

8. Bottom border design only piped with No46; press, stop pressing, pull down. Loops piped with No0 tube.

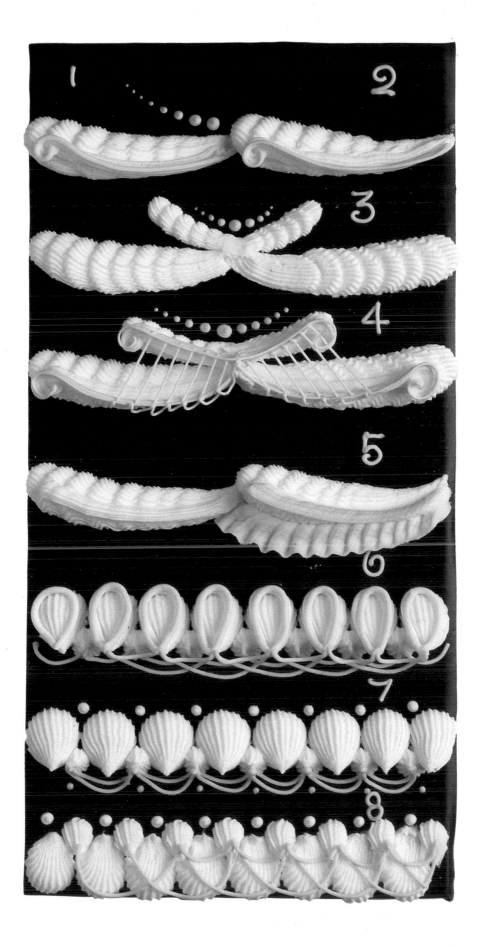

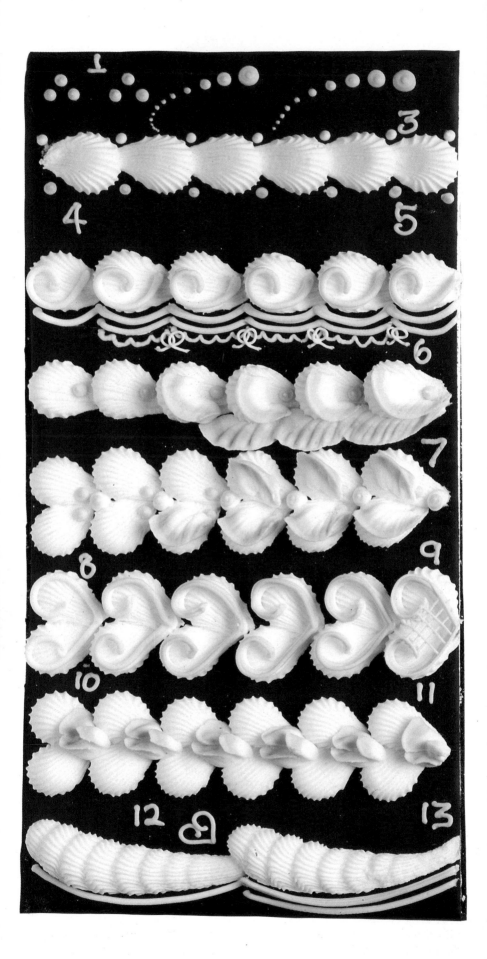

1. Practise piping dots in sets of three using a No1 tube. This exercise gives spacing practice.
2. Next pipe the graduated dots, pressing less as the dot gets smaller.
3. Shells are piped with a No46 tube.
4. Shell overpiped once in white with No1.
5. Shell overpiped with No1 and No0 tubes.
6. Shell overpiped with No59 tube; thick side of the tube touching shell, fine side upright.
7. Heart piped with No46 and overpiped with No59 with dots added.
8. Heart shape shell overpiped with No1 tube.
9. Heart shape shell plus overpiping in white with No1 and overpiping in mauve with No0.
10. Heart shaped shell piped with No46.
11. Heart shape shell with centre overpiped with No59.
12. Plain scroll piped with No46. To pipe, start fairly small, build up in centre and then ease off to finish.
13. Scroll with overpiped lines.

TRELLIS

Trellis, a traditional way to decorate a cake, is built of light lines criss-crossing each other with open squares in between. Pipe with full peak icing free of bubbles. It can be piped with any size writing tube but is usually done with No0, 1 or 2. Lines can be built up using a finer tube, each added layer building up height and shape.

PRESSURE PIPING

Pressure piping is done straight onto the surface of the cake, usually with a No1 tube.

Exercise Board 1
Heart. Press, stop pressing, pull down. Pipe left side first, then right.

Lovers' knot. Press, loop left side round, press, loop right side round.

Lovers' knot heart style. Press out a small heart sideways, then another the other way. Pipe two lines downwards.

Dots. Press, stop pressing, ease off. For graduated dots press less as they get smaller. For the smallest dot the tube should just barely touch the cake.

Dot flowers. Press, stop pressing, pull down to form a pear shape for each petal.

Birds. Press to form a pear shape for the body; press, stop pressing, pull up to form head and beak. Press, stop pressing, pull out to form wing, repeat for other side. Press wings and tail.

Swan. Pipe head and pull an S line to form breast and neck. Pipe arch for back and tail, add beak. Fill in body. Pipe an outline for the wing, then pipe loops for feathers.

Hearts. Pipe left loop then right loop. Join at the bottom.

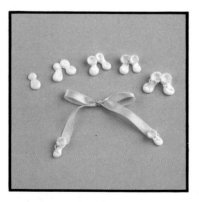

Booties and Birds
With No1 tube press, stop pressing, pull down. Press again to form side of bootie.

Pipe a second bootie.

Pipe two lines around top. Overpipe with pink.

Booties piped on ribbon bow.

Birds piped on ribbon bows.

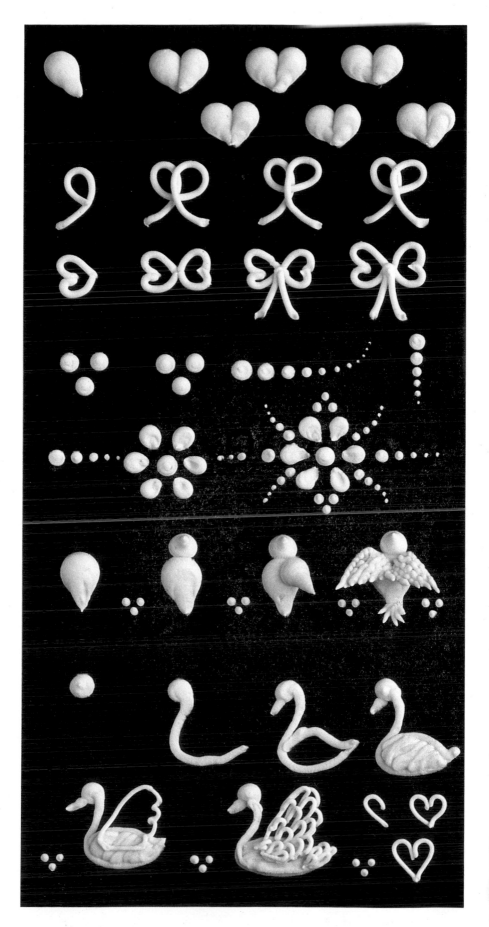

Exercise Board 2

Lovers' knot is piped first, then the birds at the base.

Swans and dots.

Hearts, kisses and dots.

Scrolls and dots.

Flowers and hearts.

Five pointed star.

Scrolls and small hearts.

38

PIPED FLOWERS

Piped flowers are made using flower tubes which go up in size from 56 to 60. The flowers are quick and easy once you learn the skill of holding and twisting the flower nail and holding the tube at correct angle. Use very firm but light icing made by adding 15ml (3tsp) powdered egg white to 50ml (2fl oz/¼ cup) water and 450g (1lb/4 cups) icing sugar. Extra egg white makes the icing stronger, lighter and it will set quickly.

Flowers that stand off the cake are made by folding the greaseproof paper in half before starting. Pipe half the flower on each side of the fold. Dry with the folded paper at a 90° angle against the side of a box or tray.

Hold the rose nail in your left hand and twist anticlockwise as you pipe one petal at a time anticlockwise. For flat flowers (all but piped roses) pipe the leaves with an anticlockwise movement also, making sure to have the wide end of the tube touching the nail and the fine side tilting up. When using a rose nail, attach the square of paper with a little icing.

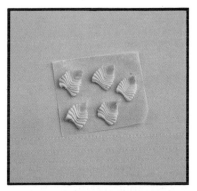

Before beginning, cut lots of 2.5cm (1in) squares of greaseproof paper. Pipe flowers and leaves onto these and then put on a tray or board for drying.

Dahlia. Rotate the nail anticlockwise while piping small close round petals. Work four layers of petals, going inwards until the centre is filled. As you reach the centre pipe smaller petals.

Primrose. Pipe anti-clockwise with the thick side of the tube touching the paper. To form a heart shaped petal use the following action: press, release, pull down, press, pull up, release. Pipe five small petals.

Daisy or Clematis. Starting at the centre of the nail pipe to the outside with the thick end of the tube touching the paper. When the tube almost reaches the out-side of the nail pull back to the centre and take off. Pipe long thin petals until the flower looks finished.

Pansy. Mix colours on a palette first, then place in the bag. Pipe two top petals anticlockwise, then one on each side. Keep the fine side of the tube tilting upwards. Pipe a yellow or brown centre.

Blossom or Forget-me-not. Rotate the nail anticlockwise; press, stop pressing, pull round. Keep the petals small and short and the flower even. Ease the last petal in and pull off.

Daffodil. Pipe six long petals; pull a paintbrush handle down the centre to make a point. Centre may be a trumpet with the same tube in a clockwise direction, or pipe three circles with a No0 tube one on top of the other. Pipe a frilled edge and stamens in the centre of the trumpet.

Lily-of-the-valley. Pipe a curved stem first, then small piped lines curving downwards. Pipe a small dot at the top and larger bulbs towards the bottom. Pipe very small dots around the base of each small bulb.

Sweet pea. Pipe the stems first and the green leaves and tendrils. With two-tone icing, first pipe the large petal at the back with the side of the tube touching the nail. Then pipe a small petal on top and a bud in the centre. The green calyx may be piped afterwards with a No1 tube.

An assortment of different piped
flowers used as top and side
decorations on cakes.

FLOWER BASKET CAKE

A simple but elegant heart-shaped
cake with a piped flower basket would
make an attractive celebration cake for
almost any occasion.

PIPED BASKETS

Piped baskets may be made in any shape using a basket nail or a small round object. Dust the mould with a little icing sugar then cover with rolled out sugar-paste in the same colour as the basket. Different size tubes may be used depending on the size of the weave. Use the same firm icing as for piped flowers. The downward line should be one size smaller than the cross line. Two colours can be used. Babies' cradles can be made in the same way.

Cover the basket nail or pot with a little flower paste.

Starting at the bottom, pipe basket weave — a long line with short lines crossing it. Pipe round the base of the basket, then the sides. Keep the tube in the same position and pipe loops to join the coloured lines.

Leave to dry overnight. Take the basket off the mould. If it doesn't come off easily it needs more drying time. Insert green sugarpaste.

The handle can be milliner's wire covered with piping. Stick it to the bottom of the basket with icing. After 24 hours when the icing is set it can be picked up by the handle.

Piped flowers on 26-gauge wire.

When dry, arrange flowers inside. In an arrangement try to have the height built up in steps on each side. Curve a few flowers over the edge. Use different size flowers plus some buds.

Below right:
Fill the basket with white sponge or white paper turned upsidedown. Cover with small piped green leaves. Stick on flowers.

Below left:
Push a handle made with milliner's wire into the bottom of the basket. Place pale green flower paste on base in which to stick the wired flowers.

Left:
Pipe basket as above. Put some sugarpaste inside and pipe small green leaves over the base. Arrange wired flowers putting buds at the top and edges with the larger flower in the centre as a focal point. A bow may be added to the top.

RUNOUTS

Runout, or flood work, is a method used to make figures, plaques, collars and borders. Any picture or design may be copied for a runout. Beginners should start with a simple shape.

Favourite children's cakes are made using runout characters copied from books or comics. Cakes with figures taken from birthday cards are fun for older children. Cuttings from newspapers or even lettering can be made in runout icing.

Runout icing is made by taking the required quantity of royal icing and breaking it down to a flowing consistency by adding small amounts of cold water, a little at a time. Paddle away the bubbles with a knife before adding the water. If the mixture becomes too runny, add some firm royal icing; if still too firm, add more water. The right consistency will come with practice and time.

With a spoon, fill a large bag about half full with runout icing. Fold in the top of the bag firmly to prevent icing oozing out, then cut a small piece from the point

the size of a tube No0 to 3. The larger the surface to be filled in, the larger the hole.

Place the chosen picture under cellophane or roasting wrap pinned well down on a soft drawing or macramé board. Outline with a fine tube. Pipe unbroken lines around the picture, then flood.

Pipe the background first, leave to dry for about 30 minutes; then pipe the foreground. A crust forms on the icing, so the outline of the foreground will be thicker giving the picture depth.

The sections you want to stand out are flooded last. Work in stages so that the picture dries out in sections for painting.

When flooding keep the point of the bag submerged in the royal icing. Take care at all times to work right up to the piped edge or border, filling in all corners and edges to eliminate air bubbles. Work icing in a circular movement to keep it even. Should air bubbles appear, break immediately with a pointed tool and pull to the edge of the design.

For the two flower plaques make the runout backgrounds, dust with colour then pipe the stems for the flowers and the lilies of the valley. Position piped roses or forget-me-nots.

Runout birds

First outline with a No1 tube. Fill in all the bird except the wing. Fill in the wing so that it stands out. Dust sky and grass background. Pipe on a branch with a No0 or 1 tube. Pipe on blossom with a No56 tube and mottled pink icing. Start painting bird. Begin with light colours and build up to the darkest. Pipe on extra icing and work in with colour and a sable brush to give a raised feather-like appearance. Completed plaque has bird stuck on with icing to give depth.

CHRISTMAS CAKE

This unusual Christmas cake features a
side design of pine trees and a runout
top decoration adapted from a
Christmas card.

RUNOUT BORDERS

Make the runout border. Outline with a No1 tube. Outline and run out flower section with No0 and fill in with fairly bold runout icing. The holly and mistletoe are flooded with pale green icing. When colour is dry paint in the flower section with a No1 sable brush, shading the holly and mistletoe. Pipe holly berries with No1 in Christmas red; when dry add a painted black spot in centre. Pipe mistletoe with No1 tube in white. When dry brush with snowflake dust.

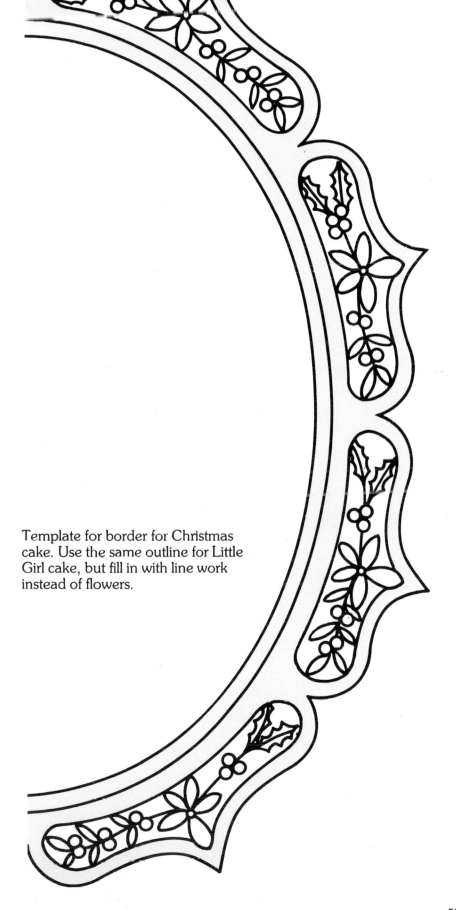

Template for border for Christmas
cake. Use the same outline for Little
Girl cake, but fill in with line work
instead of flowers.

CHRISTMAS CAKE PLAQUE

Pipe an oval plaque and fill in. Leave to dry for four days. Work with No0 tube and thick runout icing. Pipe the wheelbarrow first, doing the wheel last so that it stands out. When dry pipe mistletoe twigs all over. Use full peak beige-grey icing for the branches and pale green for the leaves. Pipe in the berries with No0 tube and white royal icing.

The mistletoe in the barrow is dusted with moss green dust.

Paint the girls in dark tones to give an old-fashioned look. Pipe the hair and scarf when dry and tone in with a damp sable brush. Dust flesh colour on the face and blend with a No00 sable brush. Pipe the lace collar with a No1 tube, then use a No0 for the outside loops.

Templates for twigs.

Side designs pressure piped directly onto the cake.

LITTLE GIRL PLAQUE

Make the runout oval plaque, piping the outline first with a No1 tube. Dry in a warm place.

Pipe the outline of the little girl with a No0 tube. Fill in with runout icing covering the background first and foreground last. Remember to let the icing dry for 30 minutes between stages.

When finished and dry, paint the little girl. Start with the lightest colour, shading the face first. Paint on the features with No00 and 1 sable brush.

Pipe the tiny rosebuds with a No56 tube whose end has been blocked with hardened royal icing. Place in the girl's hat and decorate with small green leaves.

Stick the figure onto the plaque and decorate with small dots etc.

Pipe the lace collar for the plaque as illustrated below. Dry about 24 hours in a warm place and then carefully place on plaque. Stick with icing.

Place plaque on centre of cake.

BRODERIE ANGLAISE CHRISTENING CAKE

A pretty pink and white cake with delicate broderie anglaise collars could be used for a christening, as shown, or as a birthday or anniversary cake.

RUNOUTS WITH BRODERIE ANGLAISE

Pretty broderie anglaise collars and side panels can be made in runout icing. Use patterns taken from the ornamental cloth itself or from designs found in needlework books. Use tracing paper to copy the pattern which is then pinned under cellophane or roasting wrap. The circles and ovals of the broderie anglaise pattern are piped round before flooding to leave the holes traditionally found in the lacy cloth. Stems, buds, dots and extra leaves are piped on the runout icing when firm. When the collar or panel is completely dry, fine ribbon in a pastel colour is threaded through.

Put the pattern on the runout board. Pin the cellophane or roasting wrap to the board firmly, making sure it is completely flat and even. Outline the flowers with a No0 tube, then outline the edge. Fill in, working flood icing in a circular motion from the edge, easing around flowers. Break any bubbles with a fine pointed tool. Keep returning to the starting point to avoid crusting. When finished leave to dry. Pipe a few runout bulbs on the board. These can be tested for dryness, rather than disturbing the collar.

Turn the border over onto sponge. Thread with ribbon and tie bows on the right side. Pipe lace border with No0 or 00 tube.

Leave to dry. Always complete side designs and lettering before attaching collars to the cake with firm piped icing.

CHRISTENING CAKE WITH BRODERIE ANGLAISE

Runout frame
Draw a frame on paper (an oval with a smaller shape drawn about 15mm (½in)' inside it). Cover with cellophane or roasting wrap and pin down on board. Pipe around the edges, let dry, then flood. Dry again. This frame can be used as a base for trellis work or placed on a cake with a photograph inside.

Coat cake with white icing; finish with a sharp edge. Fold and cut strong greaseproof or wax paper into eight sections and pin to cake as shown, making sure it is even with the top.

Coat bottom of cake with pink icing covering over part of the paper as well. Remove paper.

When dry pipe a frill with a No59 tube, the thick side of the tube touching the cake. Pleat as you go by moving the tube up and down. Pipe bottom shell border with a No43 tube. One row is piped up and one smaller row piped down between the shells of the first row.

Make eight sections of broderie anglaise for sides. Runout on a side of the tin used to bake the cake to get the correct curve. When dry thread with ribbon. Attach broderie anglaise side sections. Pipe bottom loop border with a No0 or 1 tube. Lace may be added with a No00 tube. Pipe lace on bottom of frill with the same tube.

Pressure pipe booties before attaching the bows.

THE CAKE DECORATOR'S BADGE

Runouts can be used to make any badge or coat of arms. Copy the symbol for a school, club or family, or design a new one, as shown in this Cake Decorator's Badge.

TO DO GO

CAKE DECORATOR'S BADGE

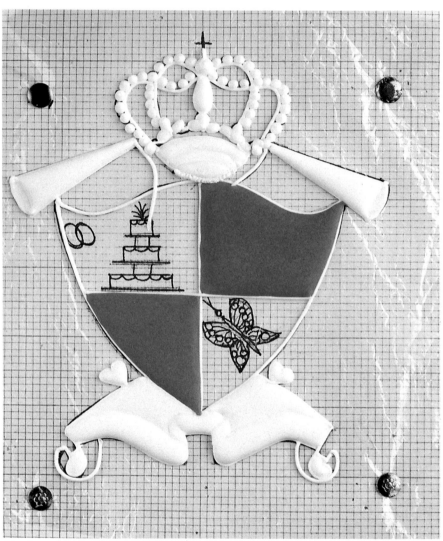

Outline the shield and icing tubes with a No1 tube. Pipe the crown and scroll section with a No0 tube. Fill in with runout icing. Pipe runout in blue icing for the two bird sections. Leave to dry. Pipe the other two sections in peach or orange. Leave to dry. Fill in scroll and crown section with runout and curved lines. When dry, build up crown with dots. Paint all colours in with food colour. Pipe the lettering with a No0 or 00 tube.

Many schools and organizations have a badge or coat of arms with a motto. These are easy to do in runout and pressure piping and make an unusual cake for a school celebration. When using a coat of arms or badge on a cake it is best to put it on a simple cake with a white background. The badge illustrated contains symbols relating to cake decoration. Icing tubes are portrayed as these are the main tools.

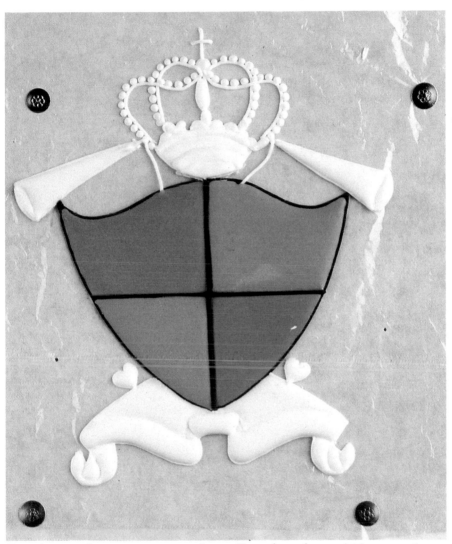

Run the motifs out, separate with a small tube and fill in with runout icing. The wings, chain, etc are done in lacework and embroidery.

Pipe the cake on with a very fine tube. Use pressure piping for the hearts below the shield.

Motifs for the badge are piped
onto wax paper. Position on the
runout badge when dry.

Template for Cake
Decorator's Badge.

RUNOUT LOVE BIRDS

Outline the birds and flood in. Using a No1 tube start piping from the beak. Try to pipe one line from beak to tail around the breast, and one line from the top of the beak over the back, to the tail. Outline four wings with a No0 tube. Leave to dry. When doves are dry turn over and flood the other side. There is no need to outline again. Dry. When dry attach the wings.

Make a heart base by moulding pastillage over a plastic heart. Leave to dry, then arrange the birds on top by placing feet in a little sugarpaste covered with royal icing. Branches and roses may be piped on the stand.

LOVE BIRDS ENGAGEMENT CAKE

An unusual engagement cake with caged lovebirds. This pretty design would also be suitable for a small wedding or an anniversary.

FREESTANDING BIRDS

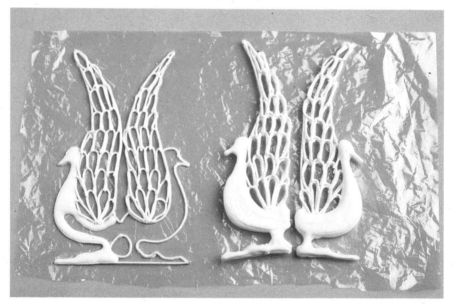

Outline the birds and wings with a No1 tube; pipe in the wings with No0 tube. Flood the head and body. Pipe two separate birds using the same pattern. When dry

turn over and overpipe the loops of the wings with a No0 tube. Flood the head and body. Leave to dry.

Prepare a 10cm (4in) round thin board with floodwork. Stand the join section on the board with icing when it is completely dry. If it does not stand firmly place some sponge at each side. Join the two birds, one at each side. Decorate with thin ribbons.

LACE

Lacework resembles crochet in many ways and the method is similar. Small drop loops are piped and built on to form different loop patterns. Use a fine tube and smooth royal icing.

Beginners should practice freehand lace loops on a practice board before attempting a cake.

You can copy any picture or design for lace. Pin the picture under cellophane or roasting wrap. Outline and fill in the design with filigree lines. If you want freestanding lace, as in wedding cake top decorations, pipe on the other side when dry. It is not necessary to outline again. When dry place on the cakes either flat or standing up.

Lace can also be piped directly onto a piped shell border.

Bells
Outline with No0 tube. Pipe the shape first and then the loop bows. Fill each bell with a lacy pattern using a fine tube. Pipe the gong with a large dot attached to the bell. Leave to dry. Small flowers piped with a No56 tube may be added.

Butterflies
Outline with No0 tube, then fill in with firm light royal icing, piping lacy lines, rounds etc. Leave to dry overnight.

Pipe the body on the cake and gently place the wings on the body. Sponge can be placed at each side until wings are firm.

LACE PARASOL

Any lacework pattern may be used for the parasol as long as all lines touch. Use any smooth ball of the correct size. Grease with white vegetable fat.

Pipe eight evenly spaced lines vertically from the top with a No1 tube. Pipe scallops to join the eight sections.

Pipe three lines in each section. Using a No0 tube, loop round on top to form a flower. Pipe four rows of loops. Pipe lines down from the centre line to join sections at the base. Pipe scallops across and at base. Pipe scallops at base with a fine tube.

Leave to dry overnight.
Turn onto sponge. It
will come off easily
when dry.

Place a small piece of
flower paste in the
centre. Pipe lines
round. Attach painted
cocktail stick with a
flower paste handle. A
bow and small rose
may be added.

FREESTANDING WEDDING BELLS

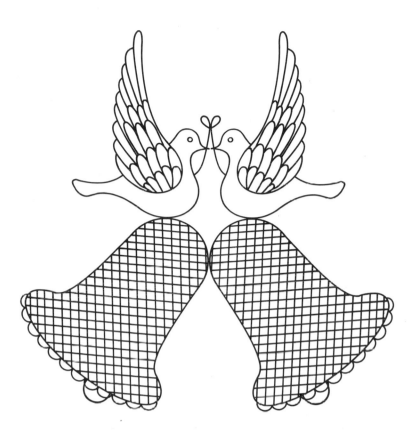

Bells: Pipe four wedding bells onto cellophane with a No1 tube. Let dry. Turn over carefully and overpipe for strength.
Birds: Pipe the birds and wings and let dry. Turn over carefully and overpipe for strength.

To assemble: Prepare a 10cm (4in) board with floodwork. Position two bells exactly opposite each other and attach with royal icing. Let dry. Position the other two bells at right angles to the other two and let dry. Attach birds on top of one pair of bells with royal icing and let dry. Decorate with wedding rings, ribbons and place piped roses under each bell.

TWO-TIERED WEDDING BELL CAKE

This two-tier wedding cake is decorated with trellis work and a trellis-work top decoration. The pillars are finished with tiny piped daisies to match the side designs.

ORIENTAL STRINGWORK

Oriental stringwork produces spectacular effects, and is not as difficult to do as it looks. Designs can be adapted from lace, knitting or crochet patterns. Oriental stringwork can be done in a single colour or in many different colours. For best results, always plan out and lightly mark on the cake where the loops are to go.

This is a method used to pipe borders on cakes using a fine tube. The cake is turned upside-down and loops are piped which will stand up above the surface of the cake. Because the cake is handled more than usual in this technique, it is best to use a firm textured cake rather than a sponge.

First turn the cake upsidedown on a firm support whose diameter is smaller than that of the cake top. Use a small cake tin or a polystyrene dummy one size smaller than the cake.

Be sure each series of loops is dry before turning the cake.

Turn the cake upsidedown and place on a support. Pipe loops from the top edge of the cake and from the shell border. Leave to dry.

Pipe another series of loops overlapping the first around the top edge. When dry, turn the cake rightside-up.

Pipe dots as shown on
the top edge.

Pipe loops to join the dots on the
top edge. Pipe another row of
loops from the shell border. The

arch of the loops should just touch
the board.

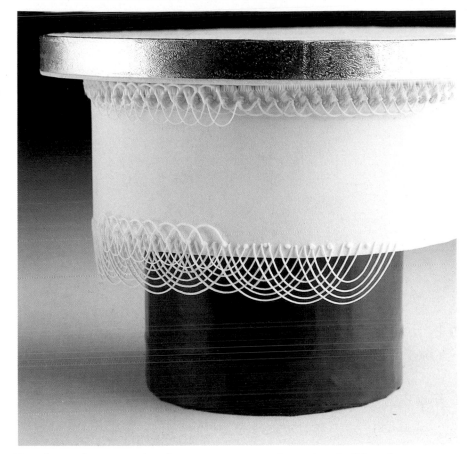

Pipe loops between the dots around the top edge, and a similar row from the shell border.

Turn cake rightside up and leave to dry before adding top and side decorations.

ORIENTAL STRINGWORK CAKE

The delicate lace parasol is a perfect complement for a cake decorated with fine oriental stringwork collar and border.

FILIGREE

Filigree is ornamental work made of fine lines formed into delicate tracery. Light, showy and fragile, it makes a cake look very special.

Place a suitable design or picture on a prepared runout board under fine cellophane or roasting wrap. Pin down, making sure the pattern is completely flat. Pipe with a No00, 0 or 1 tube, or, for heavier work, a No2.

Each piped line must touch another line or curve at some point or the tracery will break when you take it off the cellophane.

Leave to dry in a warm, dry, airy place for 48 hours before attempting to remove it from the cellophane. Do this with a very fine palette knife, pressed down towards the board.

Template for side panel.

Pipe the birds first. Outline, then fill in with trellis and loops. Pipe the butterfly in lace. Pressure pipe branches to fill the whole area. Use the pattern as a guide. Pipe flowers, buds and leaves with No1 or No0 tube, flower centres are piped with No00.

FILIGREE PANEL CAKE

Coat cake four times with icing coloured pale blue with a touch of pink; leave a sharp edge. Make two hexagonal runout borders using the templates. Outline the edge of the lace top and the sides with a No1 tube, then flood. Leave to dry.

Place the large runout border on first. Pipe a line with No43 at the centre edge, let dry. Overpipe and dry. Then add the smaller hexagonal border. When dry place sponge on three sections of the hexagonal border and rest the lace top on them. Keep the sponge small (under 15mm (½in)) and it will be easy to remove.

Pipe lines on the sections without the sponge, from top to bottom with a No1 tube. When dry remove the sponge one section at a time.

Pipe the rest of the lines the same way so that lines are now piped around the cake. Pipe lines with a No1 tube down the next border. Finish with No0 tube if wished. Add the side panels.

Pipe a line on each side with a No43 tube the same shape as the runout panel. When dry overpipe to give the effect of a stand-off finish. Carefully put each side in place.

Hold a few seconds until dry. Pipe a heart shape shell with No43 tube down the corners and add butterflies. Finish bottom board with lines piped with No1 from side panels to board. Pipe lines around plaque.

FILIGREE PANEL CAKE

This exquisite hexagonal cake is decorated completely in delicate filigree. The top design is actually a floating collar supported by fine line work.

Template for filigree top
design.

Outlines for collars for
Filigree panel cake.

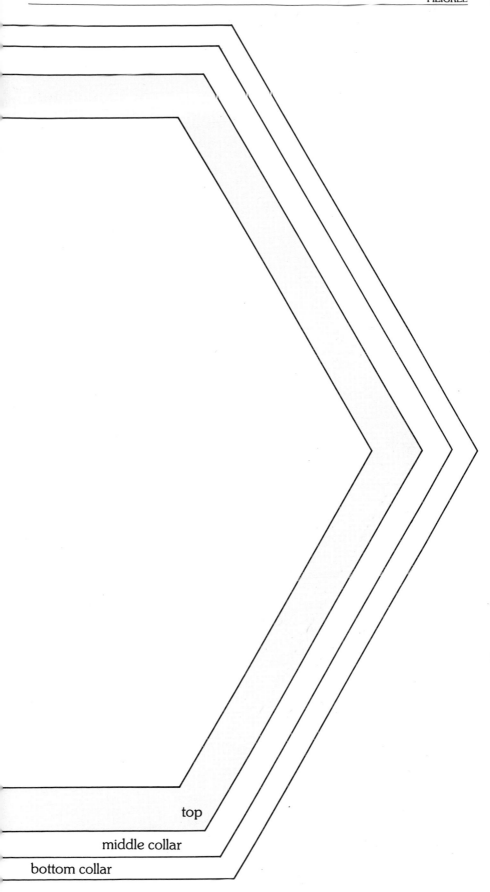

top

middle collar

bottom collar

LETTERING

The lettering illustrated is piped first with a No2 tube, then over-piped with No1. Make sure the spacing of the letters looks even, and that the writing forms part of the overall design of the cake.

When the cake is dry arrange runouts, flowers, etc before doing the writing. Use white icing as coloured icing will leave a stain if it is necessary to remove it. Over-piping can be done in a colour. Take off mistakes with a palette knife and try again.

If words are written one below the other rather than along a line it will make it easier to keep them looking straight. A scroll line can be piped below the words.

Writing in a circle

This lettering looks best when done within an 18cm (7in) circle. A centre 10cm (4in) circle is left free of lettering.

Place the cake on a turntable and pipe the uprights of the letters pointing towards the centre of the circle. If the message is long use tall, slim letters. If the lettering does not make a complete circle use scrolls to join the line.

Freehand lettering becomes easier with practice and is much more satisfactory than trying to trace or stencil the letters on the cake first.

ABCDEFGH
IJKLMNOPQ
RSTUVW
XYZ

abcdefghijkl
mnopqrstuv
wxyz

12345
67890

ABCDEFG
HIJKLM
NOPQRS
TUVWXYZ

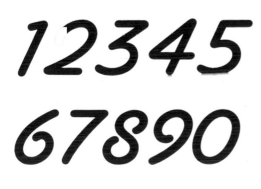

abcdefghij
klmnopqr
stuvwxyz

12345
67890

CAMEO PLAQUES

Colour the sugarpaste by adding a touch of black to pink, green or blue. Roll out the coloured paste on a little icing sugar. Make sure all icing sugar is rubbed off the surface of the paste to leave an eggshell finish.

Cut out plaques in round or oval shapes. Press the pattern from an empty perfume bottle or similar to form an impression.

Cut around plaque again as when you make the impression you will lose the shape of the original plaque. Leave to dry.

Start piping from the top of the figure (head) and press, using a bag fitted with a No2 tube and filled with normal royal icing.

Press the head round and downwards to form the neck. Pressure pipe the arms next and shape the body. Fill in.

Pipe the legs using a greater pressure for the section above the knees; the pressure is less for the lower leg and the feet.

The fine parts, such as hair, branches etc, are piped with a No0 tube.

All impression cameo figures are done in the same way; bodies filled from head to toe with No2 and the extras with a No0 tube. Plaques with other subjects, such as love birds, can be done in the same way.

Cameo plaques made using a
perfume bottle and piped, then
dusted with lustre colour.

SPORT CAKE

This unusual design features cameo-style runouts representing different sports. Other designs could be copied from photographs.

Olympic symbol reproduced with the special permission of the International Olympic Committee.

Fencing

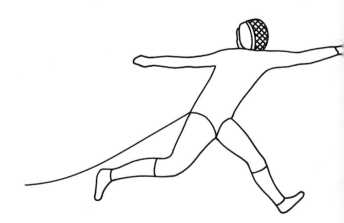

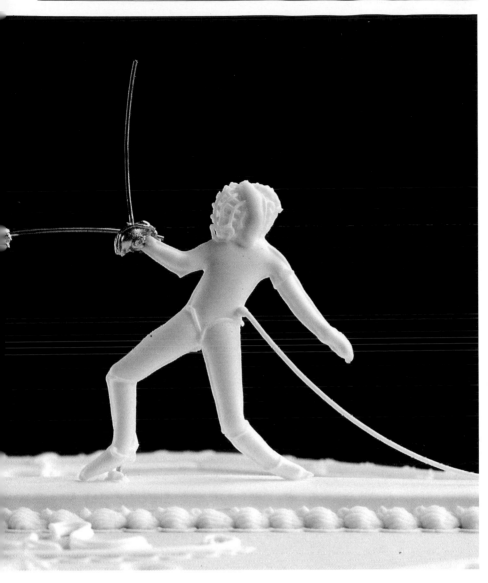

Weight-lifting

Discus throwing

Swimming

Running

Hurdling

Show-jumping

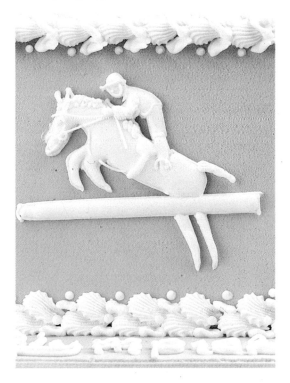

Cycling

Olympic torch

Shooting

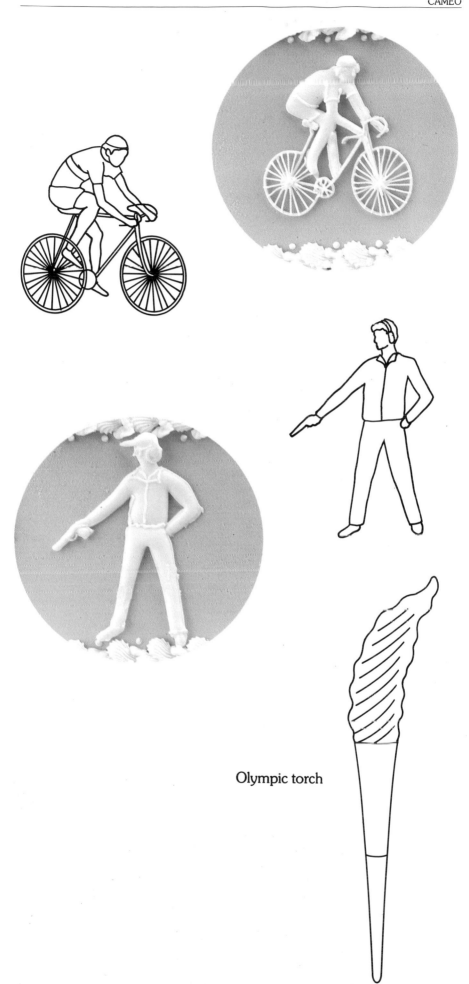

Olympic torch

Weight-lifting

Discus throwing

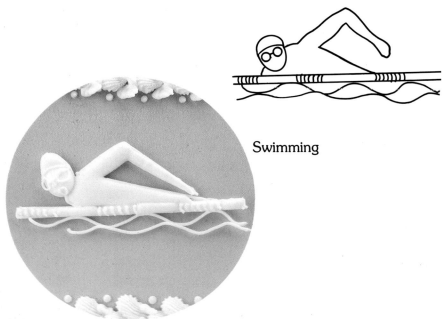

Swimming

Hurdling

Show-jumping

Running

INSTRUCTIONS FOR CAKES

Broderie anglaise christening cake. Decorate the cake following the instructions given on page 68. A photograph of the child being christened may be placed in a runout frame with lace and the name piped. Rosebuds may be added to the top with green leaves to finish.

Filigree panel cake. Directions for making this cake are given on page 98.

Love birds engagement cake.
This type of decoration, on a
much smaller scale, may be used
for the top tier of a wedding cake.
Roses can also be put under the
dome. Coat the cake with French
pink royal icing; leaving a bevelled
edge. Make runout doves as
described on page 76. Pipe writing
if wished. Make six holes in the
icing about 15mm (½in) inside
the edge for the wire. Decide the
height you want the cage and cut
three pieces of medium milliner's
wire to the desired length. Cover
the ends with white flower tape.
Place one end in a hole in the
cake and the other end in the
hole opposite as illustrated. Stick
with white icing. Pipe a line from
top to bottom with a No41 tube.
If the top of the cage isn't firm, tie
together with a little fine ribbon.
Stick on small piped blue and
white flowers. Tie a bow on top
and let it hang into cage. To pipe
the top border, pipe two scrolls
facing with No46 tube. Start at a

corner on the top; work around,
building up the scroll in the centre.
Pipe the edge; make smaller
scrolls and pull off straight in the
centre of each side. Reverse action
to do opposite side. Using a No43
tube pipe a small scroll in the
centre of each scroll. Overpipe
first using a No43 tube, then No2,
1 and 0 tubes. When dry pipe
lines in No0 tube to join the two
scrolls. Pipe bottom border the
same way. Add a frill made with a
No59 tube; the thick side of the
tube touching the cake board.
Pink and white icing is used in the
same bag, the pink at the wide
end. Next pipe the side panels
with No2 and then with No1,
making loops all around. It is
easier to pipe loops if you tilt the
cake. Finish with graduated dots.
Decorate with small roses piped
with No56. Pipe down corners of
the cake with No46 and overpipe
with No59. Pipe small blue dots
as shown.

Little girl cake. Coat the cake with a sharp edge in peach coloured icing. Make runout border for top. Pipe and flood bottom border. Let dry. Make runout plaque of little girl and attach to cake as described on page 60. Pipe on lily of the valley. Pipe a figure 18 freehand around the sides; overpipe if required.

Christmas cake. Coat the cake white on top. The sides are covered with a subtle blue-green sky and a few white clouds. White snow covers the bottom section, about 2.5cm (1in) above board. Mottled coloured icing is put on the side and the scraper pulled around over it to make the sky. When dry snow and trees are piped freehand with No0 and 1 with beige-grey royal icing. Pipe trees, fence etc as in a country landscape. Brush in snow with blue-grey wash on a No3 sable brush. Pipe a bulb border with No3 tube; red spots may be added.

Flower basket cake. Coat the cake with pale yellow royal icing; finish with a bevelled edge. Pipe the basket as described on page 46 and fill with small flowers. With No46 tube pipe a bold heart shape shell, trying to have an equal number on each side. Pipe the bottom shell in the same way. Overpipe each shell with a C shape using a No2 tube and a darker colour. Pipe top border, then bottom. Pipe loops.

Oriental stringwork cake. Coat the cake with a pale blackcurrant colour; finish with a sharp edge. Make parasol as described on page 84. Pipe a shell border around the bottom of the cake as shown. Turn cake carefully upsidedown on a support. Pipe loops as described for oriental stringwork, page 90. Place parasol on top leaning on its handle; stick with icing. Pipe oriental writing freehand on sides of cake in white.

Sport cake. Coat the cake in green icing. Make runout figures for the sides. The fencers are piped, turned over when dry and flooded on the back. Place a small piece of cocktail stick up one leg leaving 15mm (½in) to push into the cake. The sword blades are wire. When dry mask and wires are piped with No0. Place fencers in position. Pipe a heart shape shell border with a No43 tube and add dots and white leaves with No1. The five ring Olympic emblem is piped with a No2 tube. The torches are runout, both sides of the flame made of icing brushed into shape. These are added last.

Two-tier wedding bell cake. Coat the cake with pale apricot icing. Make bells as shown on page 86. Use No58 tube for daisies. Pipe trellis with No3, then 2, then 1. Pipe loops and lace. Small star is done with No43 tube. A shell made with No43 going up and No2 going down is piped on the bottom before the extension work. Pipe a loop with No2 on the side of the cake and on the board; overpipe with two lines of No1. Pipe downward extension lines with No0, finish with lace. Small rosebuds of the same colour are piped with No56. Pipe leaves. Add bells.

Three-tier wedding cake. This cake may be made without lace if wished. Make the top decoration as described on page 80. Coat top and sides of cake with white icing, leave to dry. Cut template for sides, divide into eight sections. Pipe onto the cake and coat around bottom section with pink icing. Dry. Pipe frill with a No59 tube. Two lines of lace are piped on the frill when dry. Pipe a top border of small shells with No43. Overpipe loops with No1. The bottom border is a shell piped upwards with No46 and downward with No43. Pipe loops as shown. The lily of the valley is piped straight onto the cake. Pipe roses and green leaves. Lace butterflies are added to centres as shown.